Original title:
Nebula Nonsense

Copyright © 2025 Creative Arts Management OÜ
All rights reserved.

Author: Harrison Blake
ISBN HARDBACK: 978-1-80567-821-2
ISBN PAPERBACK: 978-1-80567-942-4

A Dance amongst the Stars

In a swirl of twinkling bright,
Space critters twirl in pure delight.
With cosmic hats and shoes so neat,
They jiggle and wobble with tiny feet.

A comet sneezes, oh what a sight!
It sends the moon doing cartwheels tonight.
Stars break out in a laughter spree,
While asteroids hop like a bumblebee.

Galaxies giggle, spinning around,
As stardust sprinkles joy all around.
Jupiter juggles its moons with glee,
While Saturn dons rings for a dance, oh me!

So come take a twirl in the cosmic glow,
Where laughter and mischief endlessly flow.
In this silly realm where dreams take flight,
A dance amongst the stars, pure delight!

Celestial Carousels

Round and round the planets spin,
Swinging stars with grins akin.
Rockets jump and giggle bright,
Space-time dances, what a sight!

Saturn's rings are a hula hoop,
Jupiter's moons form a dancing troupe.
Mars trips over its own red dust,
Laughter echoes—oh, how we must!

Starry Mishaps

Comets crash in playful ways,
Leaving trails of stardust haze.
Asteroids roll like mischief's crew,
Who knew space could be this blue?

Twirling galaxies lose their grace,
Spinning wildly in this space race.
Pluto forgot where he should be,
A lost planet in a cosmic spree!

Chuckles in the Cosmos

Aliens laugh with jellybeans,
Nibbling on celestial greens.
They throw a party every night,
With twinkling lights—oh, what a sight!

Venus giggles, veils a smile,
While Mercury dances in style.
Laughter rings through the black space,
Galactic joy, a warm embrace!

Cosmic Quips and Quirks

Shooting stars throw jokes to Earth,
Tickling some with cosmic mirth.
Wormholes wink, a playful tease,
Galaxies tease, if you please!

Black holes whisper secrets loud,
While stardust forms a giggling crowd.
The universe sings a silly tune,
Underneath the giggling moon!

Orbiting Oddities

In a galaxy where giraffes float high,
Stars wear hats and comets sigh.
Planets play tag in a swirling race,
While purple aliens paint their face.

Bubbles of laughter burst with glee,
As chicken asteroids dance with a bee.
Marshmallow moons with keys to unlock,
Tickle my toes like a cosmic clock.

Deep Space Follies

Celestial clowns in a circus bright,
Juggle black holes that twist and bite.
Cosmic cats chase cosmic mice,
Riding waves of starlight nice.

Giant space fries tumble and spin,
With ketchup stars that invite a din.
Galactic gnomes on a trampoline,
Bounce past planets in a crazy scene.

Celestial Curiosities

A rocket ship with a rainbow trail,
Sails through galaxies without fail.
Kaleidoscope comets on roller skates,
Zoom past planets with giddy mates.

Quirky critters sing songs so spry,
While asteroids wink and giggle up high.
Starry-eyed dancers on cosmic floors,
Twirl and leap to echoing roars.

Quantum Quirks

In a lab of laughter, science shall reign,
Einstein plays hopscotch, avoiding the rain.
Atoms wear tutus, they prance and twirl,
While quarks are busy with a comic swirl.

Schrodinger's cat has a joke to share,
Deciding which box is the one to spare.
Physics with giggles, what a delight,
As photons dance into the night.

Interstellar Jests

In cosmic cafes, aliens dine,
Sipping comet juice, feeling fine.
They giggle at stars that dance and twirl,
In a floppy hat, a space cat gives a whirl.

With space-time noodles, they slurp and slosh,
Galactic laughter in a warm, great posh.
Black holes wear glasses, looking so slick,
Orbiting planets play hide and seek quick.

Luminous Laughter

Glowworms bounce in a celestial show,
Silly sounds echo, like 'Ho-ho-ho!'
Meteor showers rain jellybeans bright,
While rockets pirouette in sheer delight.

Planets wobble in a dance-off spree,
While comets do the cha-cha with glee.
Stars chuckle softly, twinkling, amazed,
At the goofy parade of the jovial phase.

Universe Unhinged

Quasars with mustaches, oh what a sight,
Trading bad puns under the moonlight.
Galaxies spinning like tops that are mad,
While astronauts giggle at jokes they once had.

Space monkeys swing from nebula trees,
Shouting, 'Catch the stardust, it's such a tease!'
Pulsars tickle the minds of the bold,
In this wacky realm, laughter unfolds.

Wacky Wonders of the Void

Cosmic clowns in a vacuum so bright,
Bouncing on beams of starlight, what a sight!
With humor so vast, it's hard to imagine,
Jokesters and sprites lead the great expansion.

Dancing on asteroids, wobbling with cheer,
Tripping on space dust, oh dear, oh dear!
The universe giggles, stretching its seams,
As comets race by, fueled by wild dreams.

Whimsical Wanders through Space

Stars giggle in the night,
Comets dance with all their might.
Planets spin in silly cheer,
While asteroids cluster near.

A space whale sings a tune,
Tickling moons that float like balloons.
Cosmic jellybeans pop and glow,
As warp-speed squirrels put on a show.

Mirth in the Milky Way

Galaxies swirl in a vibrant spree,
Shooting stars sip cosmic tea.
Neon aliens wear polka dots,
Playing hopscotch on cosmic spots.

Sunbeams dressed in funky hats,
Trade jokes with giggling blue rats.
Astro-bunnies bounce around,
In that twinkling, vast playground.

Playful Planets

Mars wears shades, looking so cool,
While Venus splashes in a starry pool.
Saturn's rings swing like a game,
In this lively cosmic frame.

Earth plays tag with the nearby moons,
While Jupiter cracks its funniest tunes.
Uranus bursts out into giggles,
As stardust tickles and wobbles.

Laughter of Black Holes

Black holes hide their comical grins,
Swallowing light, they pull off wins.
With a chuckle, they gobble the sun,
Making light-hearted jokes just for fun.

They twirl with stars, a cosmic dance,
Sucking in laughter at every chance.
In a space filled with giggles galore,
These jesters of gravity ask for more.

Celestial Shenanigans

In the sky where stars dance,
A cow floated by in a prance.
With a wink and a moo,
It stole my warm stew!

Planets play tag in their orbits,
Dodging space debris like little hobbits.
A comet sneezed,
And the crowd was pleased!

Alien critters throw cosmic pies,
With whipped cream that glistens and flies.
They giggle and cheer,
As they levitate near!

In this realm of wacky delight,
Galaxies frolic, oh what a sight!
With laughter so grand,
We spin hand in hand!

Spacetime Satire

A rocket tried to do a flip,
But ended up in a cosmic trip.
It twirled and swayed,
While Earth just delayed!

Martians in bow ties drank tea,
Debating the best way to flee.
A chair made of cheese,
Gave them quite the tease!

Asteroids had a disco ball,
Throwing a party, come one, come all!
They danced 'til dawn,
When the starlight was gone!

In a black hole, a jester fell,
And told a joke that rang like a bell.
Everyone laughed,
At the strange aftermath!

Lightyear Larks

Stars in spectacles read the news,
While comets twirl in shiny shoes.
A light-year giggle,
With no room for wiggle!

Saturn lost its ring in a bet,
It offered its moons, but they said, "Not yet!"
The laugh echoed wide,
As rockets all cried!

With solar flares playing charades,
Venus wore hats in many shades.
They pranced round the sun,
Laughs filled with fun!

Quasars tell tales full of jest,
In this realm, the silly are best.
So hop on this ride,
With joy as our guide!

Astral Eccentricities

Galaxies throwing cosmic jokes,
Lost in laughter, even the folks!
A planet slipped on its flip-flop,
And down the space slide, it did hop!

Constellations mime a grand play,
With stars acting silly all day.
Uranus turned blue,
At a pun it once knew!

A spaceship crafting paper hats,
Invited the sun, but he got all fat.
The orbit's a mess,
With giggles, no stress!

In this cosmic carnival bright,
Every oddity feels just right.
So let's take a whirl,
In this fun-loving swirl!

Quirky Quasars

In a dance of stars so bright,
Quasars giggle, what a sight!
Wobbling waves of cosmic cheer,
They beam their jokes from far and near.

Twinkling tales of space-time lore,
They hiccup light, and then they soar.
With each burst, a silly song,
Silly sounds where they belong.

Melodies of Mischief

In the depths of cosmic fun,
Melodies twirl, and then they run.
Planets bop to tunes so sly,
While meteroids just whirl and fly.

Mischief-makers in the night,
Twist through stars with pure delight.
Comets swoosh with joyful glee,
Making space into a spree.

Joyful Astral Anecdotes

Hear the tales from sparkly skies,
Astral whispers and silly sighs.
Stars flip words, they laugh and twirl,
While moons chuckle and softly swirl.

Galaxies have stories to tell,
Of comets tripping, oh so well.
Anecdotes of joy in flight,
Illuminating the vast night.

Floating Follies

Floating through the cosmic sea,
Stars play tricks, oh can't you see?
Galactic goofs and twinkling grins,
They frolic where the fun begins.

Planets roll like marbles bright,
Tumbling through the endless night.
A cosmic circus in the void,
Where laughter reigns, no need for coy.

Orbital Oddities

In a galaxy where socks do dance,
Planets spin in an odd romance.
Comets sneeze in a cloud of dust,
While moons giggle, as they must.

Jupiter wears a polka-dotted tie,
While Saturn cries, 'Oh me, oh my!'
Stars play peekaboo, hide and seek,
Creating chaos, oh what a freak!

Asteroids roll, looking for fun,
Searching for sunshine, away from the sun.
Cosmic clowns juggle space-time balls,
While alien cats make their calls.

Black holes spin jokes that draw you in,
With punchlines that twirl and spin.
So here we float on this cosmic ride,
Laughing loud with the stars as our guide.

Fantasy Fragments

Floating umbrellas above the blue,
Ensure the ducks wear hats, it's true!
Oranges sing while the apples dance,
In this wild, wacky, space romance.

Clouds shaped like elephants march in line,
Reciting poems about jelly and brine.
Appearing briefly for a quirk or giggle,
Bringing smiles and a cosmic wiggle.

Rainbows fly on rocket backs,
While jellybeans explode with stacks.
Space bunnies hop from star to star,
Trading carrots for candy bars.

Galactic gnomes ride shooting stars,
Chasing friendly comets and Mars.
In this funny world, let's take a seat,
Where every moment's a playful treat.

Spiraling Silly Stars

Stars twirls about in a dizzy spree,
Wearing glasses, laughing carefree.
Galaxies twist in a dance of glee,
    As planet parties spin joyfully.

Meteor showers toss candy drops,
While fluffy space llamas do the hops.
Cosmic cupcakes with sprinkles bright,
    Fill the void with delicious delight.

Celestial critters juggle and play,
On crescent moons, they laugh all day.
With laughter echoing through the void,
    As silly tales become enjoyed.

Twinkling lights burst out in cheers,
Tickling the laughs of passing spheres.
In this swirling cosmic ballet,
    Life's just a joke, come join the fray!

Whimsical Wanderings

In the land of moondust and beans,
Where nothing is quite what it seems,
Socks go sailing on comet tails,
And wobbly worlds tell silly tales.

Whirling clouds of candy floss,
Make merry music and work the gloss.
Frogs in tutus leap with flair,
As stardust sparkles through the air.

Jokes tumble down from orbiting trees,
As giggles float on a cosmic breeze.
Dreams sip tea with dandy ghosts,
While explorers laugh at what they boast.

Wander with whimsy, let laughter core,
Each star reveals an open door.
In this zany, cosmic parade,
Join the fun, don't be afraid!

Etheric Absurdities

In the sky, a pickle floats,
Wearing a hat made of stars.
Space cows dance on rainbow boats,
Baking cookies on Mars.

A frog sings songs in zero-g,
While moonbeams sip on tea.
Jellybeans grow on the moon's tree,
Oh, what a sight to see!

Galactic jelly rolls around,
Tickling comets as they zoom.
Giggly stars make silly sounds,
Filling the universe with bloom.

Silly whales in spacesuits dive,
Waving at passing asteroids.
In this fun, we feel alive,
Joyously we are overjoyed!

Cosmic Daydreams

A toaster spins in cosmic rays,
Toast flying up like shooting stars.
Planets play in zany ways,
Strumming guitars made of Mars.

The sun wears shades and takes a nap,
While asteroids play hopscotch gleefully.
An octopus leads a funny clap,
Underwater fireworks, oh so free!

Galaxies twirl in silly waltz,
As giggles echo through the void.
Space bears play tag and share a balz,
Every moment is enjoyed!

A rainbow-colored comet soars,
Tickling the tails of stars above.
In this dance, the cosmos roars,
Each twinkle whispers tales of love.

Whimsical Worlds Beyond

In a galaxy far away,
Marshmallow mountains wobble.
Kangaroos in hats at play,
Bounce through cosmic trouble.

Stars wear socks of polka dots,
Sipping juice that tastes like pie.
Clouds perform in wacky spots,
Making everyone laugh and sigh.

Aliens in bow ties prance,
Hula-hooping past the moon.
In a wobbly, silly dance,
They make a giddy tune.

Wacky worlds spin round and round,
Filled with laughter, fun, and cheer.
Whimsies in each nook are found,
Where the absurd is held dear!

Planetary Playfulness

Silly robots play charades,
In a field of twinkling lights.
Planetary fruit parades,
Dancing through the starry nights.

Glittering fish on bicycles,
Zooming past with playful glee.
Twirling in colorful miracles,
Spreading joy for all to see!

Confetti clouds rain down delight,
As laughter echoes through the void.
Each moment is a wild flight,
In a world that's unalloyed.

Frolicking under a candy sun,
Puppies wearing tiny hats.
A cosmic race has now begun,
Filled with joy and lovely spats!

Quasar Reverie

In a galaxy far, lights flicker and glow,
Aliens dance while the comets throw.
Space cats giggle at the cosmic show,
Juggling moons in a zero-gravity flow.

Asteroids swerve like they're trying to skate,
While space gnomes munch on a starry plate.
Galactic pals laugh, it's never too late,
As they bounce off the rings, it's a wild fate.

Planets in fancy hats, oh what a sight,
Singing old tunes in the dark of the night.
Shooting stars twirl, and it feels just right,
In this Quasar dream, everything's light.

Astral Antics

Comets wiggle in their shiny parade,
While planets play hopscotch, plans are made.
Space ducks quack, in a feathered charade,
Riding on rays, they dance and invade.

Meteor showers, a bubbly affair,
Crafting sweet wishes that float in the air.
Galactic giggles echo everywhere,
As they tumble and roll without a care.

With spaceships shaped like bananas and pears,
The crew all wears pajamas, no one cares.
They spin through the void, forgetting their fares,
In this cosmic playground, friendship ensnares.

Starlit Capers

Bouncing on beams from the moon's silly grin,
Cosmic critters gather, let the games begin.
With a splash of stardust, they all jump in,
As the night wraps around them like a scarf thin.

Zipping through starlight, a brave little crew,
Making popcorn planets and rainbow-flavored dew.
Giggles collide with a cosmic hullabaloo,
As they twirl through the skies, oh how they flew!

Dancing with comets, in circles they spun,
Battling light speed in a race just for fun.
In the heart of it all, no problem to shun,
Their laughter echoes, 'til the night is done.

Cosmic Conundrum

In a riddle of stars, what's the silly call?
Why did the planet go to the ball?
Wearing a tutu, looking so small,
Dancing with asteroids, having a ball.

Every black hole's a swirling surprise,
What tickles the sun? Oh, let's theorize!
With giggles and winks from the galaxy's eyes,
They ponder the wonders beyond the skies.

But time's just a joke that flips upside down,
As meteors laugh, wearing stardust crown.
Through whims of the cosmos, they spin all around,
In this cosmic riddle, joy can be found.

Cosmic Conundrums

In the void where stars collide,
Jellybeans in meteors ride.
Galactic hiccups float on air,
Why do comets comb their hair?

Aliens dance in disco light,
In spacesuits that feel just right.
They laugh at gravity's old quirk,
And moonwalk like an ancient jerk.

Planets play a game of tag,
While asteroids just laugh and wag.
A supernova's loudest cheer,
Is just a cosmic chortle, dear!

So when you look up at the night,
Just know the stars are feeling bright.
With silly games in endless space,
The universe is a funny place.

Laughter Among the Stars

In the cosmos, laughter blooms,
Wormholes spin in joyful rooms.
Saturn's rings are silly hats,
While Jupiter wobbles with laughs and spats.

Shooting stars make wishes weird,
Like ice cream that has disappeared.
Galaxies gossip, scatter and twirl,
While comets giggle through the whirl.

Tiny moons play peek-a-boo,
While black holes swirl in a funny hue.
Lightyears tickle the cosmic air,
Transporting jests, beyond compare.

So chuckle when you gaze above,
At the cosmic dance of stars we love.
Remember, humor's everywhere,
Even in the vacuum, light as air.

Astral Anomalies

Stars with sunglasses shine so bright,
While planets do the moonwalk right.
Quasars play peek-a-boo with light,
As cosmic jokes take flight at night.

Space cows float with zero gravity,
Chewing stars for their sanity.
Surreal tales of salad moons,
Rocket ships with swimming spoons.

Doing cartwheels near the sun,
Solar flares are just for fun.
Nebulas swirl in cotton candy,
Galactic giggles sound quite dandy.

In the silence, laughter grows,
Amongst the stars, a punchline flows.
So when you're lost in astral schemes,
Just chuckle at the cosmic dreams.

Eccentric Echoes

Out in space, the echoes sing,
Of rubber ducks and cosmic bling.
Alien jesters zip around,
With punchlines lost and laughter found.

A pizza floats, supreme and round,
While galaxies spin without a sound.
Silly sounds from distant light,
Make shooting stars giggle, oh what a sight!

Meteor showers drip with cheer,
Bouncing jokes from ear to ear.
Comets quack like ducks in flight,
Their tails trailing laughter all night.

So when you stare into the skies,
Remember there's fun beyond the wise.
Eccentric echoes pave the way,
For funny tales that always play.

Interstellar Improv

A Martian juggles cosmic pies,
While Venus giggles, oh what a surprise!
Stars perform a quirky dance,
In zero-g, they take a chance.

Asteroids tap their little feet,
While comets spin in wild repeat.
Pluto plays peek-a-boo with the sun,
Who knew space could be so much fun?

Galaxies twirl in their own space reel,
Black holes spinning like a cosmic wheel.
Light-years fly by with a silly cheer,
As aliens laugh, "Best show of the year!"

With laughter echoing in the void,
Cosmic antics, nothing's destroyed.
So let's toast to the starlit night,
Where silliness takes a celestial flight!

Dancing in the Ether

In the ether, a dance begins,
Space bugs twirl in sparkly spins.
Galactic grooves from a distant star,
Make everyone shout, "Don't forget to spar!"

Wormholes waltz with a jazzy flair,
Shooting stars strut without a care.
Asteroids shimmy, comets glide,
While Saturn's rings take a joyful ride.

Neptune's blues turn to techno beats,
Moonwalkers shuffle on meteor streets.
As Jupiter's storms swirl gaily around,
The cosmos hums a jolly sound.

Dance moves writhe in space's embrace,
Float like feathers in this weird place.
Join the fun, don't hesitate,
In the dance of stars, let's celebrate!

Quasar Quirks

A quasar giggles in a cosmic scheme,
 Sending out light like a wild dream.
 Galaxies tape their brightest nights,
 As pulsars play with dazzling lights.

Supernovae do the twist and shout,
While black holes spin and swirl about.
 Gravity pulls in a playful way,
Saying, "Come closer, let's play today!"

Eclipses hide, then peek-a-boo,
 Dancing shadows, oh what a view!
  Starry antics, a cosmic jest,
   In the universe's quirky fest.

With laughter echoing in the dark,
 Celestial bodies leave their mark.
So gather 'round, let's share in the fun,
 In a universe where giggles run!

Stardust Shenanigans

In cosmic dust, the shenanigans glow,
Tiny stars chuckle, putting on a show.
Planets play poker without any chips,
And black holes tease with their swirling whips.

A neutron star plays hide and seek,
While galactic clouds give a cheeky peek.
Saturn's rings toss confetti high,
As meteors zip and zoom by!

Solar flares burst with dazzling flair,
Sending giggles through the solar air.
Astrological antics, a cosmic blast,
In stardust fun, let's have a blast!

So grab your friends from near and far,
Let's join the fun under the star.
For in this chaos of interstellar play,
Every laugh lights up the Milky Way!

Cosmic Capers

Stars in pajamas dance with glee,
Planets playing hide and seek, you see.
Comets racing, what a sight,
While black holes giggle in the night.

A rocket with a toaster's cheer,
Spreading butter on a moon so near.
Aliens juggling soft cheese balls,
Laughing loudly in galactic halls.

Asteroids roll like clumsy fools,
Shooting through space, breaking all the rules.
A sunbeam tickles a distant star,
While space whales sing from afar.

Galaxies swirl in a conga line,
With meteors dancing, oh so fine.
Cosmic capers in the vast unknown,
Where laughter's echo is brightly sown.

Twinkling Trickery

Twinkling lights play tag in space,
Spinning around with a giggling grace.
A space cat chases a comet's tail,
While shooting stars tell silly tales.

Rocket mice with cheese for flight,
Zooming past in a joyful sight.
Galactic gnomes bake starry pies,
Sipping stardust with twinkling eyes.

Comets wearing hats parade the sky,
While moonbeams bounce and the planets sigh.
Cosmic pranks keep the night aglow,
With laughter echoing down below.

A black hole winked and made a spin,
Then pulled in a planet for a good grin.
Twinkling trickery fills the void,
In this universe, joy's not destroyed.

Whimsical Worlds

In worlds where marshmallows float so high,
And jellybeans rain from the candy sky.
Laughing rivers of chocolate flow,
As rainbow bridges start to glow.

Trees made of licorice sway in the breeze,
While bubblegum clouds drift with ease.
Silly critters on pogo sticks,
Bouncing high with their funny tricks.

Pineapples dance, wearing capes of gold,
As stories of whimsy begin to unfold.
Dancing fireflies with hats of cheese,
Spreading laughter like a sweet breeze.

In whimsical worlds, where dreams take flight,
Every color shines so bright.
A playful universe, a sight to behold,
In every turn, a tale retold.

Drolls of the Dark Matter

Droll creatures hidden in shadows' play,
Whispering secrets at the end of the day.
With googly eyes and floppy ears,
They share chuckles that echo for years.

Nebulous friends in a runaway beam,
Chasing giggles like a wild dream.
Gravity's jesters spin around,
Making silly sounds that astound.

Floating jokes with a twisty swerve,
Creating laughter that you can preserve.
While stars roll sobre, trying to focus,
Dark matter drolls spinning around us.

In the night, where the chuckles cut through,
Funny shadows come out, it's true.
Drolls of the dark in a playful spree,
Whirling and twirling, oh what a sight to see!

Laughing Light-years

Giggles travel far, like light,
Stars chuckle in the night.
With every twinkle, a grin grows,
Cosmic laughter in glowing shows.

Planets spin with silly spins,
Comets race, wearing grins.
Asteroids skip on dusty trails,
Navigating with chuckling tales.

Wormholes swirl like a fun slide,
Through the galaxy, joy will glide.
Constellations dance a jig,
As starlit socks get dancey big!

In a universe of bouncy cheer,
Every star makes mischief clear.
So laugh along, don't be shy,
In this vast space, let humor fly.

From Stardust to Humor

Once a speck of cosmic dust,
Now it's jokes, oh, how they rust!
Galaxies giggle, so bright at night,
Spinning yarns of pure delight.

Meteorites drop, what a sight,
Plummeting with a chuckle of fright.
Gravity pulls, but jokes hold tight,
Orbiting laughter, pure and light.

Aliens peek with a wink and grin,
In their ships, they spin and spin.
Telling tales of silly sprees,
In vast voids where no one sees.

From stardust dreams to comic beams,
Floating through the silvery streams.
Let humor drift across the skies,
In this tapestry of funny ties.

Lighthearted in the Void

In a void where silence sings,
Planets bounce on elastic springs.
Hilarity erupts from black holes,
As starlight giggles and rolls.

Shooting stars make wishes dance,
While asteroids twirl in a funny trance.
Gravity plays a trick or two,
As moons trip over the spacey blue.

Solar flares throw a laughter blast,
While comets race, having a blast.
It's a comedy show, a stellar spree,
Where even light beams twist with glee.

Floating through cosmic silliness,
Each twinkling star shares its bliss.
So join the fun, take a ride,
In this lighthearted cosmic slide!

Jovial Jotting through the Cosmos

Wandering stars tickle the sky,
With silly notes that soar and fly.
Galactic jokes ripple in space,
While meteors make a funny face.

Cosmic puns ride on solar winds,
Where laughter and orbiting friends.
Saucers of laughter glide with ease,
Sharing pie in the bright breeze.

Astrologers laugh, hair on end,
Charting giggles that never bend.
Through quasars and beams of light,
Funny planets dance with delight.

In a universe loaded with jest,
Finding joy is the real quest.
So scribble your laugh in the stars,
And let humor roam across the bars.

Celestial Jests

In the sky, a star wears a hat,
Joking with the moon, imagine that!
Saturn spins in a hula dance,
While comets giggle, taking a chance.

Galaxies twirl in a cosmic craze,
Blowing bubbles in a starlit haze.
Planets pratfall, slip and slide,
While meteors break into laughter wide.

Asteroids play tag, zigzagging free,
Winking at Venus, who's sipping tea.
Cosmic clowns with a sparkling glow,
Rehearsing jokes for the stars in tow.

Stardust tickles the Milky Way,
As shooting stars join in the play.
With every giggle, the cosmos spins,
A universe bursting with joyful grins.

Comet Capers

A comet tripped over a stardust plume,
Falling past Jupiter with a cartoon zoom.
Laughter erupts in the void so vast,
While black holes giggle at the cosmic blast.

Planets strut in their best attire,
Neptune's got jokes that could start a fire!
A meteor missed, and went 'oops' as it crashed,
While the sun chuckled with laughter unmasked.

Asteroids skate on a ring so wide,
Sharing funny tales with the galaxy's tide.
With each twist and turn, they burst out loud,
Creating a ruckus, drawing a crowd.

Those cosmic capers bring joy every night,
As stars wink brightly, a marvelous sight.
In this universe where humor collides,
A wild comedy of celestial rides.

The Great Cosmic Mix-Up

A star got lost, wandering near Earth,
Hoping to find some stellar mirth.
Planets confused, they turned around,
As the sun sang softly, a goofy sound.

A nebula sneezed in a cloud of gas,
Making the moons giggle, what a laugh!
Mercury slipped on its own shiny ring,
While Venus danced, making laughter sing.

Saturn's rings jangled, a musical tune,
While Mars tried to catch a rebellious moon.
Whirling and twirling, what a grand sight,
The whole cosmos joined in delight.

In this mix-up, the stars had their fun,
Turning stardust into jokes one by one.
Cosmic confusion makes it a blast,
In this galaxy, the laughs are vast!

Enigmatic Cosmos

What mysteries lie in this starry scheme?
Planets ponder, lost in a dream.
The sun chuckles as it lights the way,
While asteroids play tag, come out to play!

Galactic giggles echo through space,
As each star winks with a silly face.
Cosmic riddles that tickle the mind,
With comets darting, they're hard to find.

The void between worlds is filled with laughs,
As gravity pulls silly photographs.
Uranus spins upside-down, what a sight!
While black holes joke about "What's out of sight?"

In the grand expanse, where wonder abounds,
Each twinkle is laughter, in joy it resounds.
The universe whispers its happiest jest,
In the enigmatic cosmos, we're truly blessed.

Starry-Eyed Antics

A comet slipped on banana peel,
Laughing stars begin to squeal,
Galaxies dance in silly shoes,
As the moon juggles cosmic blues.

A rocket dreams of cotton candy,
While Martian chefs bake bread quite dandy,
Asteroids fall, but not with fear,
They giggle loud, then disappear.

Planets race on roller skates,
Shooting stars complain of fate,
In the dark, where laughter glows,
Cosmic giggles surely flows.

Black holes wink and play peek-a-boo,
While Saturn's rings spin tales anew,
Interstellar fun is here to stay,
In the universe's silly ballet.

Celestial Serenades

Meteors sing a tune of cheer,
While Venus clinks her glass of beer,
Galactic jesters twirl with glee,
As cosmic sounds inspire spree.

Comets play a game of tag,
Hurling giggles in a flag,
Satellites join in with a hum,
In a race where all are numb.

Stars wear hats so big and bright,
They joke about their shining light,
As worlds collide in playful glints,
Laughter echoes, soft as hints.

In the vastness, jokes will linger,
Every star is a human finger,
Strumming chords of merry plays,
In the cosmos, joy always stays.

Comedic Constellations

Orion lost his trusty bow,
Trying to capture a dancing snow,
Pisces swims with socks on tight,
Splashing water, what a sight!

The Big Dipper spills some tea,
While Canis Major laughs in glee,
Stars are twinkling, what a mess,
Constellations under duress.

A galaxy trips on its own tail,
As the universe tells a funny tale,
Eclipses chuckle with delight,
While comets prank in the night.

In this circus of cosmic fun,
Every star shines just like a pun,
Laughter soars through night's embrace,
In the vast void, we find our place.

Witty Whirlwinds

A whirlwind spins a tale of jest,
Tickling planets who need rest,
Solar flares burst out in giggles,
As Earth's inhabitants play with wiggles.

Windy whispers round the sun,
As asteroids join the cosmic fun,
Stars take selfies, count to three,
Showing off their wild decree.

Galaxies swirl in a goofy dance,
Comedic chance, a loveable prance,
Neptune grins with twinkling eyes,
While Pluto jokes about his size.

In this vast and zany space,
Humor finds its perfect place,
As orbits spin and laughter streams,
In the cosmos, we find our dreams.

Galaxy Giggles

In the cosmos, a cat plays with stars,
Chasing comets in sugar-frosted jars.
Laughter echoes through the space,
As aliens join in the race.

Planets waltz in polka dots,
While moons toss candy from tiny pots.
A rabbit hops on a shooting star,
Singing jokes that travel far.

Hubble peeks into the fun,
Spying galaxies on the run.
Jellyfish float with a silly grin,
In this dance, everyone's a win!

Wormholes twist in a silly dance,
While asteroids giggle in a chance.
In this realm of quirk and play,
The universe chuckles all day.

Astral Absurdities

Fishes fly through the twinkling night,
Wearing hats and socks, oh what a sight!
Stars wear glasses, oh, how they shine,
In this comic galaxy, everything's fine.

Asteroids juggle, while comets sing,
Bouncing off Saturn's lovely ring.
Cosmic critters spread their cheer,
With magic tricks we hold so dear.

Galactic giggles float in the air,
As meteors hop without a care.
Aliens tickle their toes with glee,
In this realm of wild jubilee!

Supernova parties light up the sky,
While planets toast with a bubbly pie.
In every corner, joy ignites,
In this zany world of space delights.

Whirling Starry Chimeras

Balloons drift past the Milky Way,
Whirling and twirling, what a play!
A cactus wears a shiny crown,
While unicorns dance all around.

Clouds shaped like mustaches float,
As sunbeams sway, giving a quote.
Pigs on rockets zoom in delight,
Making wishes every night.

Galactic beans brew cups of fun,
As they sip stardust under the sun.
Fluffy rabbits with moons for ears,
Crack up the cosmos, bringing cheers.

In this absurd, whimsical spree,
Cosmic chaos is the key.
Spinning in laughter, round we go,
In a universe of gardens aglow.

Cosmic Doodles

Stars sketch laughter on dark blue slides,
Whimsical doodles on cosmic rides.
A dancing cupcake spins with glee,
As planets giggle in harmony.

Saturn's rings are a jump rope game,
While funny meteors join the frame.
A penguin sings a song so bright,
Tickling funny bones, oh what a sight!

Spaceships wear bowties and dance the night,
Jokers orbiting with pure delight.
Cartoon comets make silly faces,
As they zoom through outer spaces.

In the galaxy's colorful parade,
Everything's silly and laughter's made.
With every twinkle and cosmic cheer,
Dreamy doodles sparkle here!

Celestial Chuckles

In the vastness of space, a cat flew by,
Wearing a hat, oh my oh my!
Stars twinkled brightly, giggling so loud,
As planets wobbled, feeling quite proud.

A comet sneezed, what a sight to behold,
Spreading stardust, shiny and gold.
Asteroids danced, doing the twist,
In a cosmic party, who could resist?

Saturn's rings spun like a hula-hoop,
While Martians joined in, forming a troop.
They juggled moons, what a clever feat,
Floating through space, still staying on beat.

In the end, they all fell to the floor,
Laughing so hard, they couldn't do more.
Galactic joy spread across the sky,
Where the fun never ends, oh me, oh my!

Cosmic Curiosities

Aliens brewed coffee on Jupiter's red,
With marshmallow clouds above their heads.
Sipping stardust with giant straws,
Bursting with laughter, oh, what a cause!

Pluto threw a party, just to feel bold,
Inviting the comets, bright and gold.
Everyone danced in a zero-grav scene,
Giggling and swirling, like a dream machine.

Asteroids played tag, zooming around,
Creating a ruckus, what a strange sound!
Quasars wiggled with a cosmic cheer,
While space whales hummed a tune in their ear.

They all shared jokes about black holes,
Who could resist those whimsical rolls?
So if you peek into the night,
You'll see them dancing, a comical sight!

Ethereal Laughter

Bubbles floated near a starfish bright,
Telling tales of a mischievous night.
Where rockets wore socks and space boots too,
While Martians played cards with a ghostly crew.

Satellites giggled at silly old Earth,
Spinning round in a dance of mirth.
One lost a signal, oh what a fuss,
As meteors screamed, "Don't ride that bus!"

A galaxy joined in a sing-song spree,
With notes made of light, so wild and free.
Fish in the sky wore tutu's bright,
Twisting and twirling in pure delight.

Falling star wishes were tossed in the air,
As moonbeams chuckled with an elegant flair.
Laughter echoed far, through infinite space,
Join in the fun, and let joy embrace!

Light-Year Larks

Buzzing through time, a spaceship whirred,
Chasing a comet that just had occurred.
"Where's my coffee?" yelled a robot from school,
While asteroids snickered, calling him a fool.

Aliens raced on pogo sticks near,
Sky-high jumps filled the void with cheer.
Each hit a crater with a bounce and a boom,
As laughter erupted, filling the room.

Wormholes twisted in colorful swirls,
As swirling moons giggled, dancing like girls.
Nebulas teased with their fluffy embrace,
Tickling starlight in a comical chase.

Blasting through giggles in every quadrant,
Light-years of humor, oh how grand!
So if you find joy in the starry expanse,
Join the larks, and let laughter enhance!

Silly Supernovae

In the night sky, stars play hide and seek,
They twirl and dance, so goofy and chic.
A burst of colors, a cosmic flare,
Laughter echoes through the inky air.

Comets slide by on roller skates,
As planets gossip about their mates.
Silly aliens with wiggly feet,
Throw galactic parties, oh what a treat!

Starfish hang out in zero gravity,
Sipping stardust, feeling all savvy.
They twinkle with joy, a sparkling cheer,
In this vast cosmos, there's nothing to fear.

So here's to the jests that the stars throw,
A celestial circus, a cosmic show!
In the depths of space, let's join the spree,
Laughing with light-years, just you and me!

Celestial Imagination

In a sky full of dreams, where giggles ignite,
Planets wear hats of the silliest height.
With stars as confetti and moons as the cake,
We'll feast on the clouds, what a joyride to make!

A spaceship shaped like a giant shoe,
Zooms past the sun, oh what a view!
Martians play tennis with glowing green balls,
As laughter and stardust rain down the halls.

Galaxies swirl in a chaotic dance,
Space critters giggle, they love to prance.
Jumping from asteroid to shiny new star,
With every leap, they travel so far!

So bring on this joyride through realms of delight,
Where imagination sparkles, oh what a sight!
In this cosmic playground, let spirits roam,
The universe chuckles, we're never alone!

Constellation Capers

Connect the dots, it's a puzzle divine,
Where bears wear hats, and stars brightly shine.
Oh, look at that lion, he's tickling the moon,
While fish play the banjo to a cosmic tune.

A mishmash of critters in twinkling lines,
Dancing to rhythms of old starry vines.
With every new cluster, a tale comes alive,
The universe chuckles, it's how we survive.

Asteroids juggling in a grand circus act,
While shooting stars perform tricks, oh so intact.
The dragon next door is knitting a star,
Creating a blanket to cozy up far.

So grab your imagination and take to the skies,
Join in the laughter where starlight flies.
In this constellation of whimsical dreams,
We'll share in the joy, or so it seems!

Hello from the Void

In the silence of space, there's a tickle of mirth,
As comets grow curious about planet birth.
A vacuum of giggles where jokes float around,
With echoes of laughter, and silliness found.

Wormholes are portals for the quirky and fun,
Transporting the wacky like it's just begun.
A chicken on Mars with a top hat so grand,
Declares a grand dance, it's a galactic band!

Invisible friends are the best kind to keep,
They whisper and chuckle, and never will sleep.
With dark matter chuckles and gravity's grin,
Life in the void is where nonsense begins!

So wave to the stars as you twirl in the breeze,
In this cosmic café, you can do as you please.
As we drift through this emptiness, join in the jest,
For in this grand nothingness, we are truly blessed!

Jests of the Milky Way

In the galaxy's spin, a cow jumps high,
With a lasso of stars, it floats by.
Aliens giggle, the cows wear hats,
Mooing in rhythm with cosmic spats.

Planets are pies, we'd take a slice,
But watch out, they're flipping, not so nice.
A comet sneezes, boogers fly,
Asteroids dodge, or they'll surely cry.

Rings of Saturn shimmer and sway,
As moon mice dance at the end of the day.
Each twirl a burst of glittering flair,
Even black holes chuckle, pulling them there.

So grab your rocket, let's zoom and spin,
In this goofy universe, let's all dive in.
Laughter's the fuel, so fill up the tank,
For space silliness, we've no need to prank.

Cosmic Whimsies

Jupiter's storms play hide and seek,
With giggles exploding, they're far from meek.
Saturn's rings, a pet's playful chase,
All the stars join in this merry race.

Pluto, the dog, barks loud from afar,
While distant comets wish upon a star.
They twirl and whirl in an endless dance,
Each pulse of laughter, a merry chance.

Stars wear pajamas, their twinkle so bright,
As meteors zoom in a flash of light.
Above, the space critters jive and prance,
In this cosmic circus, they take a chance.

Chaos reigns, but it's all in cheer,
For every black hole brings friends near.
With a whoop and a whirl, they play all night,
In this wacky cosmos, it's pure delight.

Starlit Paradoxes

A puzzle in space, oh what a sight,
A one-eyed alien juggling with light.
He fumbles with planets, they spin and roll,
While supernovas giggle, filling the hole.

Galaxies swirl in a great big mess,
Each star a jester, causing distress.
The moon trips over its own glowing tail,
As it tumbles through shadows, we laugh and wail.

Quasars quirk, with their beams so bright,
Sending silly signals, day and night.
A cosmic comedy, cosmic smiles,
Even the void cracks jokes all the while.

With laughter and whimsy, we bound through the dark,
Electricity pulses, sparking the spark.
This universe plays, day after day,
In endless absurdity, we find our way.

Celestial Fool's Play

In the cosmic playground, we slide and swing,
Comets are kites, let's launch them, zing!
Asteroids play catch, with stars in their eyes,
While the sun shines brightly, not one surprise.

Planets wear glasses, pretending to read,
Galactic novels, oh what a deed!
With a wink and a nod, they share tales grand,
Of space-time fables, not just bland.

Saturn's kids giggle, making a mess,
Sprinkling stardust, oh what a stress!
But all in good fun, so don't you fret,
For laughter in space, we'll never regret.

So bring out your joy, your cosmic delight,
In the theater of stars, we dance overnight.
With every chuckle, the universe sings,
In celestial play, oh, what fun it brings!

Galactic Giggles

In a comet's tail, they ride the breeze,
Laughing with stars, and doing as they please.
Jumpy asteroids do a silly dance,
While planets trade jokes in cosmic romance.

Little green critters wear hats that are tall,
Telling jokes to the moon, they have a ball.
With asteroid pies flying through the night,
Each bite is a giggle, a pure delight.

Big aliens juggle with stars in their hands,
While quarks make confetti in colorful bands.
They twirl and they spin, clever little sprites,
Creating a ruckus, bringing joy to the nights.

When cosmic winds carry their ridiculous cheer,
Even black holes chuckle, they can't help but leer.
In this silly space circus, laughter's the rule,
Where every bright sparkle's just playful and cool.

Whims of the Universe

A squirrel in a spaceship is chasing a star,
While Martians are playing guitar from afar.
The moons are in hula-hoops, spinning around,
Making the cosmic circus so joyfully sound.

Shooting stars slip on banana peels bright,
While the sun hums tunes that feel just right.
Galaxies giggle as they twist and twirl,
While comets wear bows like a fancy girl.

Asteroids roll like marbles on the scene,
And cosmic dust bunnies hop 'round pristine.
Each twinkle a wink, a mischievous tease,
Inviting the stargazers to laugh with ease.

Nebula creatures with purple and blue,
Send tickling tickles right down to me and you.
With each burst of light comes a chuckle or two,
In the whimsical playground, where dreams always stew.

Starlit Jamboree

In a galaxy bustling with bright neon sights,
Rovers dance silly under shimmering lights.
Shooting stars tumble, bumping off each other,
While a group of comets play tag, oh brother!

Dancing on craters, the little green guys,
Juggle space snacks, they've got quite the size.
Saturn's rings sing a tune sweet and grand,
While Jupiter's storms offer laughs unplanned.

Interstellar squirrels tap dance on the moon,
While echoes of giggles play a sweet tune.
And just when you think it all can't get better,
A black hole joins in, wearing a party sweater!

So come take a dive in this cosmic delight,
Where laughter and joy paint the vast starry night.
With each playful bounce, your heart starts to soar,
In this starlit jamboree, there's always more.

Fantastical Fables

Upon the bright canvas of dark velvet skies,
Stories are woven, just watch as they rise.
Where space-faring turtles with monocles glance,
At whimsical clouds that start doing a dance.

Rabbits with rockets wear capes made of cheese,
Zoom past the planets with whimsical ease.
They chuckle as they flip through their fables pure,
Finding laughter in tales that will always endure.

The sun and the moon make a switch for a day,
While shadows and light start to frolic and play.
A giant made of stardust tells tales of delight,
Painting giggles in the sky, like fireflies at night.

With each quirk of fate and each twinkling tale,
The wonders of laughter unfailingly sail.
So gather your dreams, let your worries unfurl,
In this playful universe, let's laugh and twirl!

Humor in the Heavens

Stars wearing hats, what a sight,
Saturn's rings twirl, just out of spite.
Moonbeams giggle, dancing in glee,
Jupiter's storm shouts, "Come play with me!"

Galaxies spin, like kids on a spree,
Mars plays hide-and-seek among the debris.
Comets slip on cosmic banana peels,
While black holes eat up all the meals!

Asteroids toss cake at aliens near,
While the sun winks, with a mischievous cheer.
Shooting stars giggle, racing through space,
In this wacky void, we all find our place.

The cosmos is wild, with laughter and fun,
A riot of joy, shining like the sun.
Space is our playground, silly and bright,
Join in the laughter, it's all out of sight!

Astral Antics

Pluto plays tag, but no one's it,
Venus is blushing from a cheeky comet.
Uranus chuckles, rolling with glee,
While the Milky Way pours milk in its tea.

Stars are not far; they're behind a veil,
Throwing funny jokes, and it's never stale.
Neptune's cool, with shades on its face,
Laughing at Earth in this silly race.

Celestial cats chase lunar cheese,
While satellites dance in a cosmic breeze.
Aliens prance with their green little feet,
Hosting a party with galactic treats.

Asteroids giggle, tumbling in flight,
Wishing on wishes, oh what a sight!
Take a ride on this cosmic surprise,
Where humor resides in the stellar skies!

Celestial Absurdism

In the sky, a cow jumps in glee,
Chasing a dragon, sipping sweet tea.
Stars juggle planets, a comet's on fire,
The universe laughs at its own wild choir.

Eclipses wink, and starlight pirouettes,
While odd creatures dance with no regrets.
Celestial giants play hopscotch in time,
Chanting silly rhymes, oh what a clime!

Galactic jesters tickle the moon,
Spinning nebulas with a silly tune.
Each planet grins, wrapped in a cloak,
Of cosmic giggles, bursting like smoke.

Laughter echoes, with no end in sight,
Painting the cosmos in whimsy and light.
So grab a seat for the celestial show,
Where absurdities bounce, in the galaxies' flow!

Cosmic Caprice

Stars in sunglasses, strutting around,
Dancing down craters, without a sound.
Spaceships giggle, flying with pride,
While comets tease, like a cosmic slide.

A sunbeam prances, a playful sprite,
Tickling the planets with pure delight.
The moon hula-hoops with rings of bright light,
While galaxies swirl with all of their might.

Astrological clowns juggle the night,
Painting the sky with colors so bright.
Quasars blast jokes that make meteors fall,
In this cosmic circus, we're having a ball!

So let's laugh together, both near and afar,
In this wild universe, we're all a bit bizarre.
Caprice and humor rule the vast space,
Join in the fun, in this stellar embrace!

Starlit Surrealism

In the night sky, cupcakes float,
With sprinkles bright, they softly gloat.
Astronaut cats in hats so tall,
Dance on moonbeams, having a ball.

Space squirrels with acorns of gold,
Tell wild tales that never get old.
Jupiter laughs, while Saturn sings,
Creating joy with cosmic flings.

A comet slips on slippery cheese,
While planets sway in the cosmic breeze.
Galaxies twirl in a goofy trance,
In the universe's silly dance.

Stars wear pajamas, twinkling delight,
As shadows frolic in the soft light.
And who needs gravity's heavy weight,
When laughter spins beyond the great?

Laughter Among the Stars

Giggles bounce from Mars to Venus,
As asteroids join the fun, oh, genius!
Alien clowns with big floppy shoes,
Juggle black holes, what a wild muse!

Meteor showers turn into confetti,
As space whales waltz, oh-so-pretty.
Planets play tag, they zoom and glide,
While the sun chuckles with pride.

A rocket ship filled with jellybeans,
Zooms past Saturn's hula hoop scenes.
Each star a smile, dancing so free,
In a cosmic carnival, joyfully.

Rainbow comets paint the dark void,
Where shimmering laughter is never destroyed.
In this universe, so fresh and bright,
Humor shines like the purest light.

Cosmic Mystique

Stars brew potions in a cosmic cafe,
With laughter that brightens the milky way.
Galactic elves with glittering wands,
Slinging good wishes across the bonds.

Asteroid races with jellybean fuel,
Making space travel a whimsical school.
With rockets fueled by tickles and cheer,
Every journey brings fun, never fear.

Whirling around in a playful spin,
As planets giggle with every win.
While cosmic dust tickles your nose,
The universe winks, and that's how it goes.

Stargazers shuffle in funny delight,
Laughing at pixels that dance in the night.
With every twinkle, a chuckle anew,
In the cosmic quilt where the laughter grew.

Whirlwind of the Cosmos

In a whirlwind of colors, stars play hide and seek,
With cosmic giggles that twinkle and speak.
Planets toss marshmallows, fluffy and round,
While moons twist and twirl, joyfully unbound.

The sun throws confetti with rays of pure fun,
Celebrating life, screaming, 'I'm number one!'
Uranus spins jokes no one else hears,
In the laughter of galaxies, allay your fears.

Meteorites speed, with a slide and a dash,
While cosmic clowns make a colorful splash.
A dance of the cosmos, bright jaws agape,
In the spiral of joy, oh, what a landscape!

Stars break into chuckles, orbiting tight,
As laughter erupts in the soft, velvet night.
In this silly ballet where nonsense takes flight,
Every twinkle and giggle feels just so right.

Cosmic Whimsy

In a jar, a comet floats,
Wearing socks and silly coats.
Dancing with a laughing moon,
Chasing stars, they'll be here soon.

Galaxies spin their playful tricks,
Silly asteroids play with sticks.
Planets giggle, roll and play,
In a waltz of bright ballet.

Saturn's rings like hula hoops,
While stardust forms a band of loops.
Cosmic cats with tails like tails,
Chase the echoes of their tales.

On a comet, a party's due,
With space cake and cosmic stew.
Join the dance, give it a whirl,
In this fun, peculiar world.

Starry Paradox

Two stars argue, who shines bright?
One says, 'I'm the twinkling light!'
The other laughs, 'Oh dear, not so!
I'm the one that steals the show!'

Planets whirl like spinning tops,
Jupiter just can't stop his hops.
Venus joins, a silly spin,
While Mars plays hide and seek with sin.

A galactic conga line appears,
Comets shimmy, stifling cheers.
Dark matter wants to join the fun,
But trips and falls — oh, what a run!

Tickling black holes, watch them giggle,
As a supernova starts to wriggle.
Stars collide in fits of joy,
While space-time wobbles like a toy.

Celestial Nonsense

On the sun, a picnic's set,
With burgers that you can't regret.
Martians bring their famous fries,
While space-dogs bark at passing pies.

Uranus offers minty shakes,
While asteroids bake in sprawling cakes.
Saturn's rings are forks and spoons,
As meteors play festive tunes.

Cosmic owls wear pajamas neat,
Telling jokes that can't be beat.
Stars roll over, laughing loud,
As solar wind flips the cloud.

Slapstick comedy in orbit spins,
With hidden laughter and cheeky grins.
In this void, silliness blooms,
As joy echoes through cosmic rooms.

Galactic Riddle

What's a star's favorite falling game?
Catch a comet, shout the name!
Jupiter laughs and takes a leap,
While Saturn winks, a secret to keep.

Why did the moon bring a map?
To find the stars that love to nap!
Nebulas prank with colors bold,
Creating shadows, stories told.

Asteroids giggle, 'Knock, knock' says one,
While other space rocks have no fun.
Inside the riddle of the night,
Lies a question, shining bright.

What's the answer, you may ask?
Silly mysteries are the task.
In the cosmos, riddles roam,
Making stars feel right at home.

www.ingramcontent.com/pod-product-compliance
Lightning Source LLC
Chambersburg PA
CBHW051638160426
43209CB00004B/705